THIS IS ME! 2022

A COLLECTION OF POETRY

Edited By Reuben Messer

First published in Great Britain in 2022 by:

Young Writers
Remus House
Coltsfoot Drive
Peterborough
PE2 9BF
Telephone: 01733 890066
Website: www.youngwriters.co.uk

All Rights Reserved
Book Design by Ashley Janson
© Copyright Contributors 2022
Softback ISBN 978-1-80015-977-8

Printed and bound in the UK by BookPrintingUK
Website: www.bookprintinguk.com
YB0504S

FOREWORD

For Young Writers' latest competition This Is Me, we asked primary school pupils to look inside themselves, to think about what makes them unique, and then write a poem about it! They rose to the challenge magnificently and the result is this fantastic collection of poems in a variety of poetic styles.

Here at Young Writers our aim is to encourage creativity in children and to inspire a love of the written word, so it's great to get such an amazing response, with some absolutely fantastic poems. It's important for children to focus on and celebrate themselves and this competition allowed them to write freely and honestly, celebrating what makes them great, expressing their hopes and fears, or simply writing about their favourite things. This Is Me gave them the power of words. The result is a collection of inspirational and moving poems that also showcase their creativity and writing ability.

I'd like to congratulate all the young poets in this anthology, I hope this inspires them to continue with their creative writing.

CONTENTS

Hamstead Junior School, Great Barr

Reece Rattu (11)	1
Dhiren Chauhan (10)	2
Aum Soni (11)	4
Abdulrahman Kareem (11)	5
Laurence Oppong (11)	6
Roshni Dubay (11)	8
Elyza Garfield (11)	9
Fatima Din (10)	10
Jayden Rowe (10)	11
Emmanuel Blake (10)	12
Sonam Kailey (10)	13
Yusuf Imaan (11)	14
Michael Allen (11)	15
Tinashé Hall (10)	16
Isabel Humphries (10)	17
Lloyd Oppong (11)	18
Suraiyah Safdar (10)	19
Amina (10)	20
Michelle Oluwo (10)	21
Freya Read	22
Arjan Bhatia (11)	23
Sean Reid (10)	24
Gurleen Singh (11)	25
Oliver Ellis (10)	26
Edward Mondoy (10)	27
Amrita Rai (10)	28
Ethan Harman (10)	29
Bobby Atkiss (10)	30
Mariah May Mulcare (10)	31
Genet Abebe (10)	32
Jasmeen Singh (11)	33
Mankirat (10)	34
Bahast Omar (11)	35
Connor Johnson (10)	36
Aman Sahota (11)	37
Zuzanna Pitera (10)	38
Scarlett Lee Mason (11)	39
Noah Peacock (10)	40
Tia Hathaway (10)	41

Mary Elton Primary School, Clevedon

Elliot Everhard (9)	42
Bella Murray (9)	44
Lacey Neath (8)	45
Eloise James (9)	46
Isabella Finnie (9)	47
Harper Steven (9)	48
Eva Ware (9)	49
Chloe Tilley (8)	50
Archie Powell (8)	51
Rafe Crawshaw (8)	52
Snowbelle Wright (9)	53
Bence Kollat (9)	54
Lucas Ball (8)	55
Oliver O'Brien (8)	56
Willow Puul-Tonkin (9)	57
George Casey (9)	58
Jasmine Bessant (8)	59
Jessica Galloway (9)	60
Jacob Holland (8)	61
Esmae Dance (8)	62
Charlie Spriggs (9)	63
Caelan B Eccles (8)	64
Matilda Pavey (9)	65
Michaela Hodge (8)	66
Josh Sweet (8)	67
Ronnie Sadler (8)	68

Toby Ward (8)	69
Frankie Flack (9)	70
Ella Buttery (8)	71
James Pearce (9)	72
Olivia England (8)	73
Indiana Badger (8)	74
Evie Gully (8)	75
Hollie Hepworth (8)	76
Sienna Gomm (9)	77
Andrew Liu (8)	78
Jaden Cox (8)	79
Charlie Henley-Smith (9)	80
Megan Greenway (9)	81
Keeley Johns (9)	82
Finley Barrow (8)	83
Maddie Upton (8)	84
Sam Barney (8)	85

Old Hall Primary School, Brandlesholme

Ruby Pilling (10)	86
Saraih Jakeway-Couser (10)	87
Dylan de Jager (11)	88
Eliza Goodier (11)	89
Max Lindley (10)	90
Zach Mehers (11)	91
Shuraim Khan (11)	92
McKinley Haslam (10)	93
Harry Nolan (10)	94
Charlotte Goldsbrough (10)	95
Jackson Brown (10)	96
Harry Nuttall (10)	97
Zayn Sultan-Smethurst (10)	98
Rocco Sharpe (10)	99
Matilda Rose Hargreaves (10)	100
Isabella Anne Lord (10)	101
Ava Challender (10)	102
Faziah Ahmed (11)	103
Mollimae Brown (11)	104

Smarden Primary School, Smarden

Isabel Quinn (8)	105
Rosie Gray (7)	106
Pearl Crowe (7)	107
Lizzie Waldock (7)	108
George Etheridge (9)	109

St Cuthbert's Primary School, Glasgow

Sofia Kowal (9)	110
Patience Asemota (9)	111
Jenna Chi (9)	112
Macy Louise Green (10)	113
Elizabeth Aiwekhoe (8)	114
Sara Carbin (9)	115
Nadia Cudjoe (9)	116
Aleksander Jagielski (9)	117
Michael Odigie (10)	118
Tyler Redmond (9)	119
Lennon Brereton (9)	120
Lily Mae Gurney (8)	121
Martins Omonijo (8)	122
Kingsley Odigie (8)	123
River Warren (8)	124
Declan Atkins (8)	125
Tiernan Warren (8)	126
Hevar Karimi (8)	127
Hanna Rekas (8)	128
Lacey Sutherland (8)	129
Sophie Morgan (10)	130
Lexi Stewart (8)	131
Darren Docherty (8)	132
Charlie Clarke (8)	133
Keira-Rose Mullen (8)	134
Jack Chen (8)	135
Poppy Johnston (8)	136
Junior Hendren (9)	137
Milena Bednarz (7)	138

Westwood Primary School, Leeds

Hollie Longbottom (9)	139
Jon-Paul Massey (10)	140
Sienna Faith Thornton (9)	141
Lacey Mai Prince (9)	142
Chloe Mead (10)	143
Charlie Smith (8)	144
Imogen Cardiss (9)	145
Casey Marie Clements (10)	146
Peter Folkes (8)	147
Alfie Beanland (9)	148
Fabian Bundy (11)	149
Freya Ward (9)	150
Alfie Opie (11)	151
Riley Smith (9)	152
Koby Lucas Bransberg Kirk (8)	153
Mia Rush (9)	154
Myles White (10)	155
Xavier Mead (7)	156
Porchia Last (7)	157
Carter Prince (7)	158
Charlie Green (7)	159
Abbie Burdon (7)	160
Isla Cockcroft (7)	161
TreydenThomas Appleyard (7)	162
Tisha Z Kakunguwo (7)	163

THE POEMS

Lost But Found

It all started with a slight change,
But soon, it developed and morphed into a perilous monster,
He hides it, but he knows he can't for long,
Thinking people will judge him,
He walks about school, thinking they are judging him,
It slowly engulfs his crippled emotions and feelings.

He wakes up and meticulously gets ready for school,
Focusing on every detail of his appearance,
He looks in the mirror,
Repeatedly seeing a disappointment,
He knows it's all on his head, but-
The 'voice' pulls him back in.

Soon he realises it was too, too much,
Tells his closest people,
He may breathe a sigh of relief,
And live life to the fullest.

Reece Rattu (11)
Hamstead Junior School, Great Barr

Boy In The Savannah

There once was an adventurous boy,
Who lived a life of joy,
He had a gift to talk to animals,
He is the boy in the savannah.

The boy raced with the antelopes,
Down hills and up slopes,
Fed with the giraffes,
Happy with all the laughs.

There was a dark place where not an animal would cross,
Full of dead plants and bones and moss,
There was an evil lion who roamed that terrain,
Face-to-face with him and you will feel a world of pain.

The boy in the Savannah tiptoes to the centre of the dark land,
With fear he stood waiting,
The beast walked in as the boy was trapped and could only stand.

His mane was as brown as his eyes,
His fur was as golden as the stars,
And his claws as sharp as knives.

The boy smiled and so did the lion,
The lion licked the boy and kicked him on his back,
The lion was somehow friendly and didn't attack,
They galloped through the Savannah and the boy has lots of friends, now another,
Now we know not to judge a book by its cover.

Dhiren Chauhan (10)
Hamstead Junior School, Great Barr

Life Is Hard

L ove series are weird, which is why I don't binge,
I also hate holes in paper, it really makes me cringe.
F orget about that now, let's talk about TV,
E very time I come home, all I have to do is clean.

I never get to watch TV, unless I'm a good boy,
S ay I'm really, really good, I might get to play with a toy.

"H ey, will you help me?" that's all my mom says,
A nd if I try to escape with a lie, my life she analyses,
R ight now I'm sitting in my room, hoping for a good dream,
D ownstairs I hear clattering, probably another cleaning scheme.

This is me!

Aum Soni (11)
Hamstead Junior School, Great Barr

I Want To Be A Millionaire!

When I grow up and become a millionaire,
I'll buy a massive mansion for me and my family to share,
I'll sit in my backyard, enjoying the sun,
While I watch my kids in the pool, having fun,
I will buy an enormous boat, no wait, a cruise,
And I will play sports all day, hoping not to lose,
I'll teach my kids boxing to make them big and tough,
And I will buy them whatever they want until they've had enough,
I'll give money to every charity every once in a while,
And in the morning, me and the kids will run a mile,
But before all of that, I have the lottery to win,
And I think the chances of that are very slim.

Abdulrahman Kareem (11)
Hamstead Junior School, Great Barr

My Imagination

I opened my eyes,
A crystal emerges from the clear blue sky,
I felt like in two worlds,
The wind swirled,
The crystal opened its light,
I saw something which was quite white.

The robots were having a battle,
They made a lot of cattle,
I closed my eyes and opened them back up again,
I was in a zoo full of animals!
Monkeys are running around,
Wow, there were a lot of sounds.

I cleared my mind,
But I was in my worst fear, heights,
It felt like I was rock-climbing,
I was scared,
I was terrified.

I felt like I was falling down,
I woke up and I was happy it wasn't real.

My imagination!

Laurence Oppong (11)
Hamstead Junior School, Great Barr

No Planet B

I went on a walk and what I saw,
Were people drunk and smoking, disobeying the law,
Nicotine called, saying, "Come, use me!"
And in the forests they're cutting down the trees,
Just so you know, there's no Planet B!

I don't know if there is a chance,
Destruction is taking a glance.
A bright future, I cannot see,
Us humans will have to beg and plea.
Just so you know, there's no Planet B!

But if we work together, we can make change,
There might be a way, we can break the chains.
We could be able to take death's lead,
Just so you know, there's no Planet B!

Roshni Dubay (11)
Hamstead Junior School, Great Barr

Welcome To A Fairy-Tale World

Welcome to a fairy-tale world where there are fairies and elves,
In castles, the potions sit on the shelves,
Look at the talking trees,
Go in the room of doors which actually doesn't have any keys,
Make a wish with a special apple,
Come with me into a fairies' chapel,
In the mountains the dragons breathe fire,
As Jack's beanstalk grows higher and higher,
Old goblins under the ground,
A world where dreams are found,
People with power good and bad,
No one ever gets mad,
I wish this world was real,
I know it isn't real, I don't know how I feel.

Elyza Garfield (11)
Hamstead Junior School, Great Barr

The Foolish Young

The day I existed,
The day the world twisted,
Pitch-black turned everything Mom insisted,
As I start to grow,
My genes show,
I laugh and play,
On the computer every day,
Mom, wait for this,
Mom, wait for that,
The things I regret,
The things I want to take back,
When I was younger,
I was reckless,
I looked at the older kids and thought they had everything,
I'm embarrassed about who I used to be,
But I'm proud of who I am now,
I have not achieved what I wanted to achieve,
But I've achieved something better,
This is who I am.

Fatima Din (10)
Hamstead Junior School, Great Barr

This Is The Life Of Me

The world I live in,
It's full of possibilities,
Some days are light,
Some days are dark,
Sometimes all of them leave a mark,
The days and nights get longer every day,
The times creep up on me, it's very clear to see.
This is the life of me.

The world I live in,
Is sometimes in darkness,
The time has come to say,
It's time for the darkness to go away,
And set the light in my heart free,
And show me the possibilities,
This will help me to learn,
To know,
This is the life of me,
This is the life of me!

Jayden Rowe (10)
Hamstead Junior School, Great Barr

I Love Minecraft

My favourite character is Minecraft Steve,
I have wings that are made from leaves, I hate creepers and zombies,
So, when I kill one, I shout... *Whee!*
I play Minecraft on PS4,
So, when I kill the Ender Dragon, it lets out a mighty *roar!*

My least favoured character is Herobrine,
Probably because he has an eerie shine,
When I see him, I don't feel fine,
As my lifeline begins to decline,
Some people step out of line,
So enter the villain, Herobrine.

That's it, my favourite game; I know that game through its fame.

Emmanuel Blake (10)
Hamstead Junior School, Great Barr

A Girl's Life

Every single day, I build up who I am,
A million and one dreams are filling up my head.
Living with the motto; dream big dreams,
Only a middle-class girl, yes, that's what I said!

Happiness is what I strive for, not for perfection,
Drawing every day, that's what I do,
Cooking, dancing, singing and there's more,
Never holding back and that is true!

I'm a girl boss, yes, that's true
An engineer, that's what I'm going to be,
Living in a fun life, mischief and fun,
And completing my dreams because this is me!

Sonam Kailey (10)
Hamstead Junior School, Great Barr

My Heroes

Spider-Man leaps through a metal jungle,
Ichigo shouts, giving us all chills,
The more I watch, the more I fall down this tunnel,
Why am I so run-of-the-mill?

But that's the thing about superhero stories,
There's always a background that's oh so gory,
For Ichigo's mom and uncle Ben are still dead,
That's the human I relate to when I'm down in my head.

So whilst I see these people with admiration,
Sometimes you have to understand,
Having a human relation,
Is what really makes a 'super-man'.

Yusuf Imaan (11)
Hamstead Junior School, Great Barr

Caleb Mark Allen

C ute as a button,
A dorable little delight,
L ovely little ball of joy,
E nchanting little baby boy,
B eautiful little child who is loved by all.

M onster of the house,
A ngry little baby when he gets annoyed,
R are little soul that is like an angel,
K id, he hopes to be a smart kid.

A bsolutely a great football player,
L uxury cuddles when he is happy,
L ittle chubby-cheeked baby,
E xquisite,
N ice, he is a kind little soul.

Michael Allen (11)
Hamstead Junior School, Great Barr

Monster And Me

Me and my best friend,
Our friendship will never end,
Through thick and thin,
Outside or in,
It's just me and my best friend.

Whether he's a monster or not,
Dribble or snot,
We play together, we laugh together,
I will be your best friend forever,
It's just me and my best friend.

I will be there for you,
Even when you're feeling blue,
When you're happy or sad,
Or when you just feel bad,
It's just me and my monster best friend.

Tinashé Hall (10)
Hamstead Junior School, Great Barr

Positivity

Find happiness in every day,
Even if you have to look harder,
Practice self-love daily,
To become better.

Never give up on your dreams,
And love haters,
Because if they say rude things,
They won't get attention.

I know it's hard,
But never give up,
Dream big dreams, wish on stars,
To never get scared.

Take a step back,
Reflect on your day,
They can't be flowers without rain,
So make people happy today!

Isabel Humphries (10)
Hamstead Junior School, Great Barr

Dodgeball Star

Ah, dodgeball, one of my favourite sports,
It's fun, it's amazing!
It feels like a gift,
My throws are fast as lightning,
I'm happy about who I am,
I have long arms and I am very tall,
Even though I lost many times,
We all learn from our mistakes,
I was a lion every match,
I love every moment of dodgeball,
The ball goes *whoosh!*
Once, I got the PE teacher out!
I'm really good at dodging,
Maybe I will become a dodgeball champ.

Lloyd Oppong (11)
Hamstead Junior School, Great Barr

Best Friends

B est friends are really the best,
E verything is better with them,
S ometimes may argue with you,
T alk to you for ages,

F lower together,
R eady to help you whenever,
I n the end they always are inspiring,
E ncourage you to do better,
N ever will stop caring,
D epend on you when life gets challenging,
S upportive friends will stay with you until the very end!

Suraiyah Safdar (10)
Hamstead Junior School, Great Barr

What Makes Me!

Dancing around my living room,
Singing in the steamy shower,
Shining the golden diamonds,
Twisting my long and silky hair,
Rainbow unicorns dancing around,
Glistening glitter dazzling around like a wondrous flame,
This is me!

I'm funny,
I'm kind,
I'm caring,
I'm brave,
All that matter's is that everything stays the same,
Looking like a star up on stage, singing till my last breath I hold.

Amina (10)
Hamstead Junior School, Great Barr

Amazing Acrostic Poem

M om says I'm manipulative, but I don't see it.
I nteracting with others is my favourite hobby.
C onfident about myself, I know I'm fabulous.
H onest to whoever asks, why would I lie?
E very fibre of me is full of positivity.
L azy in bed, but who can blame me?
L ovely at school, that's what all my teachers say.
E nergetic every day, that's how life should be.

Michelle Oluwo (10)
Hamstead Junior School, Great Barr

Cold, Calming Forest

Welcome to the forest of love,
Where there's everything, even a dove,
Come here to calm down,
When you've got a bit of a frown,
This forest will make you warm,
Maybe even make you yawn.

This forest has a waterfall,
Which is very colourful,
There are lots of bees,
Which make you get down on your knees,
This is the beautiful, blooming forest of love.

Freya Read
Hamstead Junior School, Great Barr

Ways Of Life

Is this where you resign in life?
Sadness will stab you with a knife,
Getting so, so sad,
Will turn you mad,
Such a happy place.

Where do you go when sad?
Somewhere happy?
I will go somewhere gladly,
Are you somewhere happy?
Such a happy place.

Red roses are blue, for me,
And you,
I think to myself,
What a wonderful world.

Arjan Bhatia (11)
Hamstead Junior School, Great Barr

Who I Want To Be

I want to be a chef,
I think I am the best,
I have loved cooking since I was nine,
I name the food as mine,
I love cooking so much! I want to do it without my mom by my side,
My favourite food to eat is lasagne,
I think of it all the time in my mind,
Hopefully, I can make it in a restaurant,
A restaurant that will be mine,
This is me!

Sean Reid (10)
Hamstead Junior School, Great Barr

To My Mommy

She is the best at everything,
She is excellent,
She is more than anything to me,
Whoever does everything is her,
I can't appreciate how much she has done for me.

She is like a diamond,
You are the most precious thing ever,
She is the one who motivates me,
Whenever I feel sad,
She will make me smile,
Who could it be?

Gurleen Singh (11)
Hamstead Junior School, Great Barr

My Holiday

Brothers and sisters piling into the minivan,
I wonder where we are playing, staying and where we can read,
Destination one, the smell of the salty sea slaps me in the face,
Whilst the sun beams down on us,
Seagulls awake at our arrival,
The holiday begins,
It's time for a picnic, grab some blankets,
So full of sandwiches on the plates.

Oliver Ellis (10)
Hamstead Junior School, Great Barr

My Favourite Things

I am smart,
I like maths,
My favourite subject of my class,
I want to be an engineering architect,
My favourite sport is football,
I like playing games,
Try something new for me,
Travelling around the world,
Never giving up,
Helping around the house and school,
Trying my best always,
I love drawing, it's my thing!

Edward Mondoy (10)
Hamstead Junior School, Great Barr

My Imaginary Friends

I close my eyes,
And in my head,
Rainbows are placed here and there,
But my favourites are the monkeys in disguise,
All the worries disappear,
When I see them fly,
They go very, very high,
When I go somewhere else I realise that worries are no longer here,
I can't leave without them,
My imaginary friends!

Amrita Rai (10)
Hamstead Junior School, Great Barr

The GOAT (Cristiano Ronaldo)

R onaldooo! And he scores!
O h my days! It's Ronaldo!
N o chance for the defenders,
A nd he scores!
L oss for the away team, they just couldn't stop Ronaldo.
D ear me, he was humiliated by Ronaldo.
O hh and Ronaldo scores! He beats Pele's goal record!

Ethan Harman (10)
Hamstead Junior School, Great Barr

What I Do When I Feel Sad

When I feel sad,
I'm really not sure what to do,
It always seems to be that I've done something bad,
When I'm with my friends I'm usually very happy,
Also very chatty,
Also when I'm alone,
I haven't got much tone,
So I need to speak more,
So don't let me be torn.

Bobby Atkiss (10)
Hamstead Junior School, Great Barr

My Bestie

She is kind,
She is caring,
She is brave,
She is funny,
She is my bestie.

She is different,
She is strong,
She means the world to me,
She is my bestie.

She is like a box of chocolates with different surprises inside,
Guess who she is,
My bestie is Tinashe.

Mariah May Mulcare (10)
Hamstead Junior School, Great Barr

I Love To Draw

I love to draw,
Drawing is special,
Drawing is my art,
I would draw all day,
Drawing is what I do.

I add detail when I draw,
Because that is what,
I do best.
When I draw it reminds me of my,
Memories.
Drawing is my hobby because drawing,
Is what I love to do.

Genet Abebe (10)
Hamstead Junior School, Great Barr

What Inspires Me

I am a girl,
Who is eleven years old,
Who likes singing as well as cooking,
Nothing calms me down,
Except singing,
I am a girl,
Who never thinks she will never be a singer,
But I have to keep pushing myself,
And never give up until I complete my dream,
And sing on stage.

Jasmeen Singh (11)
Hamstead Junior School, Great Barr

What Zodiac Sign Am I?

My element is fire,
I'm a confident leader,
Don't tell me to calm down,
No, I'm not a clown.

The planet I rule is Mars,
I may battle Scars,
The birthstone of mine is diamond,
Sadly I won't leave.

Who am I?

Yes, my star sign is Aries!

Mankirat (10)
Hamstead Junior School, Great Barr

My Favourite Things

Football's my favourite sport,
Cristiano Ronaldo is my favourite player,
Pizza is my favourite food,
Neymar is one of my favourite players,
BMW is my favourite car,
Manchester United is my favourite team,
Orange juice is my favourite drink,
White is my favourite colour.

Bahast Omar (11)
Hamstead Junior School, Great Barr

Furious Beast

I am angry,
I am mad,
I am arguing,
I am sad,
I am rad,
I am impatient,
I am red,
That's what I said!
I am a furious beast,
Without fear, I don't struggle,
I get up on my knees when I'm in trouble,
I never bow my head to someone who hustles.

Connor Johnson (10)
Hamstead Junior School, Great Barr

My Favourite Sport

F ierce games of football,
O ccurring on a pitch,
O perations, you will need,
T ackling these players,
B rought my team the victory,
A man you can do this,
L imping off the pitch,
L ook at me now!

Aman Sahota (11)
Hamstead Junior School, Great Barr

The Noble Nature

N ature is sweet, nature is soft,
A lily dances with tenderness and love,
T rees singing a sweet tune,
U p and above the skies are blue,
R ose as sharp as a sword in use,
E dges and hedges as nice as you.

Zuzanna Pitera (10)
Hamstead Junior School, Great Barr

This Is Me!

I am loud, I am proud to be the person I am,
I am kind, I am helpful whenever I get the chance,
This is me!

I am kind, caring and I love sharing,
I am willing to help when it's needed,
This is the life of me!

Scarlett Lee Mason (11)
Hamstead Junior School, Great Barr

My Aspiration

You play this game every day,
You can't mistake how it's played,
You kick a ball from side to side,
You let it fly in the sky,
If you're lucky you will succeed,
And I will indeed!

Noah Peacock (10)
Hamstead Junior School, Great Barr

My Favourite Sport

I am really sporty,
I like to play football, sometimes I hurt myself,
I never give up,
I always train in my spare time,
When I'm older I hope I make it.

Tia Hathaway (10)
Hamstead Junior School, Great Barr

Elliot's Life Of Fun And Other Things

E lliot loves maths,
L ikes books, hates spiders,
L ikes kingball and netball too,
I s clever and kind,
O ften plays football,
T alks a lot,
S illy with friends.

L ives in a happy home,
I f sad sits alone,
F un every day,
E very moment is amazing.

O ver and over it's school again,
F lies to an imaginary maths land.

F uture will bring fun things,
U sing my Nintendo,
N ever lying.

A bout that maybe not so true,
N ever does wrong,
D id nearly die.

O ther than that time flies by,
T ell your secrets to trusted people,
H elp friends with stuff,
E veryday fun things, happy,
R ead this stanza again.

T allies up height,
H elps with jobs,
I n a world of fun things,
N ever needs help,
G iving to charity,
S o I have a fun life.

Elliot Everhard (9)
Mary Elton Primary School, Clevedon

My Favourite Things

B lue, blue is my favourite colour, blue is the colour of the sky, sea and all of my things.
E lephants, elephants are my favourite animal, elephants are big, loud and cute, I love elephants.
L una is my favourite character from Harry Potter, Luna is funny, Luna is cool, Luna can see things, Luna makes me more confident.
L augh, I like to laugh, I like to make people laugh, laughing makes me happy, laughing with my friends is the best.
A nimals, animals are the best, my favourites are pandas and elephants, animals are funny and smart.

Bella Murray (9)
Mary Elton Primary School, Clevedon

What Ingredients Make Me

What you will need to make me:
Animal jam, messiness gel, dance power, laziness sprinkles, cheese and ham,
Pizza, Harry Potter sugar, friendly flour, sporty flour,
A lot of crazy, fun sprinkles, weird powder, laziness sparkles,
Egyptian powder, happiness sugar, drawing king powder,
You will need nothing else.
Steps:
Five tablespoons of animal jam,
Five sparkles of laziness,
Animal jam, weird powder and laziness,
A dash of everything else,
Bake for forty-five minutes,
Let cool down,
Sprinkle drawing icing.

Lacey Neath (8)
Mary Elton Primary School, Clevedon

Kindness Rocks

K indness is the best feeling,
I ncredible and awesome,
N ot being a bully feels good,
D on't bully, you're hurting people's feelings,
N ever spread rumours that aren't true,
E pic, awesome kindness,
S uper smiles and cool kindness,
S miling is the best.

R umours don't do kindness,
O f course it's okay to be kind,
C ool kindness and happiness,
K indness is the best in the world,
S uper epic, super cool!

Eloise James (9)
Mary Elton Primary School, Clevedon

The Recipe That Makes Me, Me!

This is me, kind and helpful,
This is me, friendly and grateful,
Silly, crazy, confident,
But that's what makes me, me.

I also am a story writer,
But also I love learning,
Animal lover, Harry Potter lover,
But that's what makes me, me.

I may be sensitive,
But also am collaborative,
Happy all the time, clumsy,
But that's what makes me, me.

I am exciting but caring,
Thoughtful, smart,
Loving but curious,
But that's what makes me, me!

Isabella Finnie (9)
Mary Elton Primary School, Clevedon

Recipe To Make The One And Only Me

To make me you need:
A teaspoon of confidence,
A jug full of happiness,
Pinch of excitement,
Tablespoon of comedy,
A litre of curiosity,
A sprinkle of kindness.
What you need to do:
Mix the teaspoon of confidence with the jug full of happiness,
Add the pinch of excitement and stir softly,
Add the tablespoon of comedy,
Mix the litre of curiosity,
Add the sprinkles of curiosity and stir roughly,
Put in the oven for fifteen minutes then leave to cool.

Harper Steven (9)
Mary Elton Primary School, Clevedon

Eva Loves Horses

E va loves chocolate brownies,
V icie is my squishmallow,
A nd I love horses.

L ove animals,
O n horses like my favourite horse Barney is when I am most happy,
V icious,
E va is my name,
S ometimes annoying.

H appy and kind,
O n a horse all day,
R iding is the best,
S ometimes a bit sad,
E va loves football and karate,
S uper amazing and fantastic.

Eva Ware (9)
Mary Elton Primary School, Clevedon

What Ingredients Would Make A Recipe

I would have animals on my cake.
I would put a picture of me on my cake.
I would put candles on my cake.
I would put candles of a number on my cake.
I would put some sprinkles on my cake.
I would put some chocolate cherries on my cake.
I would put a picture of me playing a board game with my dad on my cake.
I would put a picture of me painting.
I would put a picture of me and Charlotte with our baby sister on our cake.
I would put my family on my cake.

Chloe Tilley (8)
Mary Elton Primary School, Clevedon

Smart And Cheeky

S mall and creative,
M indful and mysterious,
A rtistic and smart,
R ight and respectful,
T houghtful,

A nd,
N aughty,
D oing the right thing,

C ats are my favourite animal,
H e is a black cat,
E ating all day
E ating all times,
K ind and wonderful,
Y awning in the morning.

Archie Powell (8)
Mary Elton Primary School, Clevedon

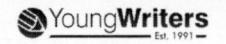

Recipe Me, I Am Rafe

I am Rafe,
I am cheerful,
Dependant, smart and a genius.
I think I am better than everyone,
When I'm not better than everyone in the world.
But I am courageous, curious, collaborative,
Silly and funny.
I like football,
I'm really good at it.
Also, I am polite, generous and happy.
I'm always excited for everything,
And also I'm exquisite.

Rafe Crawshaw (8)
Mary Elton Primary School, Clevedon

What Makes Me, Me

S now is my nickname but my name is Snowbelle, this is a poem about myself.
N etflix I never get tired of, my favourite show is 'Floor Is Lava'.
O rganised, I am very organised, I hate when things are messy, I think they should always be neat and tidy.
W inter is my favourite season because January is in winter and my birthday is in January, that is why.

Snowbelle Wright (9)
Mary Elton Primary School, Clevedon

What Characteristic Makes Me

If you walk by I will give you a smile,
I can make you laugh if you want it,
If you're feeling down I'll help you have a laugh,
I will stand up for you if you're sad or struggling,
And I think you're nice.

What am I?
If you want to do the chores I say, "Hey, do you need help?"
If you're crying I will give you a helping hand.

Bence Kollat (9)
Mary Elton Primary School, Clevedon

That's Me

A gingerbread man,
A spoonful of confidence,
Five pounds of fun,
Ten pounds of comedy and mischief,
Melted chocolate with sprinkles of fun,
A football,
A bottle of annoying,
A pizza,
A video game cake,
A bottle of skill,
A peach for skin,
Chocolate for hair,
Bake in the oven for seven minutes,
Done, that's me.

Lucas Ball (8)
Mary Elton Primary School, Clevedon

The Grand Acrostic Poem Which Makes Me

T he thing that makes me is that I'm kind,
H appy all the time,
I love my family,
S ome of my hobbies are about nature.

I 'm ready, respectful and safe,
S taying together with my family.

M e working hard,
E veryone like me has friends.

I'm the kindest me!

Oliver O'Brien (8)
Mary Elton Primary School, Clevedon

Pet Lover

P ets are great,
E specially the fluffy ones,
T he ones that have no fur can still be loved,

L ove even the nocturnal ones,
O ver the not nice ones,
V ery nice still,
E ver and forever love them,
R eptiles are my first joint first favourite animal, especially bearded dragons.

Willow Paul-Tonkin (9)
Mary Elton Primary School, Clevedon

I Love Football

F ootball is my favourite game,
O ffside! My goal didn't count,
O MG! He's better than me,
T o the pitch I go to destroy,
B ut I'm just a kid,
A ll and all,
L osers over there, I win again,
L OL! Another killer assist, I got as much as a real football player.

George Casey (9)
Mary Elton Primary School, Clevedon

This Is Who I Am!

J umping is fun,
A mazing,
S mart,
M akes things because it's fun!
I ndividual,
N ice,
E ager.

I ndependent
S ometimes silly.

C ool,
R eally friendly,
A lways me,
Z oo is fun,
Y ay! Too fun.

Jasmine Bessant (8)
Mary Elton Primary School, Clevedon

This Is Me!

T his is me, kind and happy,
H elping is what I love to do,
I ndependent is my middle name,
S miley, sporty and smart are all things I am.

I s anyone in need of a friend?
S o come to me, I'll help you through.

M e is who I love to be...
E ventually.

Jessica Galloway (9)
Mary Elton Primary School, Clevedon

Be Confident

C onfidence is cool,
O range is a cool colour,
N othing can stop you when you are confident,
F riends forever,
I t will be okay,
D ifferent things to do every day,
E very day is cool, when you add confidence,
N ever give up,
T ennis is a cool sport.

Jacob Holland (8)
Mary Elton Primary School, Clevedon

How I Feel

H appy I always feel like,
A nd still not old enough but it's average,
P laying, oh the thing I love,
P laying and dancing every day to night,
Y ear by year and I am still happy as always.

M any times I smile, I lose count,
E ar is listening while smiling.

Esmae Dance (8)
Mary Elton Primary School, Clevedon

In Loving Football

F ootball is my favourite sport,
O MG! I am loving football,
O ffside! I am so mad,
T hree goals in one match,
B ut I've lost no games,
A m I going to be an amazing player?
L OL, I am amazing,
L OL, I am fantastic.

A professional player.

Charlie Spriggs (9)
Mary Elton Primary School, Clevedon

What The Letters In My Name Stand For

C ub,
A friendly boy,
E ager to build Lego,
L ikes doing woodwork,
A ctive,
N ever lets you down.

E pic,
C lever at maths,
C lever at coming up with stories,
L ikes cooking,
E nergetic,
S leepy.

Caelan B Eccles (8)
Mary Elton Primary School, Clevedon

This Is Me!

Harry Potter is something I like,
I also like to ride my bike,
Me and my friends are really funny,
I really like porridge with honey,
I adore drama school,
I think it is really cool,
I like Horrible Histories,
And I like to solve mysteries,
As busy as a bee,
I love all my family.

Matilda Pavey (9)
Mary Elton Primary School, Clevedon

Me!

K ind to everyone,
I ncredible at drawing,
N othing stops me,
D elish food that I make.

M ischievous me,
E lectricals smart as the internet.

F un things that I do,
U p and energetic me,
N utty jokes that I say.

Michaela Hodge (8)
Mary Elton Primary School, Clevedon

I'm Josh

J olly, jovial Josh
O utstanding sportsman
S uper speedy striker
H appy when I go bowling

S killed at football
W heelie king on my bike
E ggs - love them boiled
E xpert at scooting
T op player at goalkeeping.

Josh Sweet (8)
Mary Elton Primary School, Clevedon

Remarkable Ronnie

R un as fast as a cheetah
O utside games are my favourite things to do
N ow I'm eight I can ride a bike one-handed
N o one can beat me at running
I enjoy playing football with my friends
E ating delicious pepperoni pizza is my favourite meal.

Ronnie Sadler (8)
Mary Elton Primary School, Clevedon

Toby's Life

K nights are cool,
I got cubs on Thursday
N ever negative,
D ads are kind.

S ailing on a boat is fun,
I like to play with Lego,
L ikes playing rugby,
L ikes playing tennis,
Y outh club is fun.

Toby Ward (8)
Mary Elton Primary School, Clevedon

How To Make Me!

A spoonful of happiness,
Ten kilograms of giggles,
Thousand kilograms of sleeping sprinkles,
Sushi,
Animal love,
Thousand kilograms of gaming dust,
Music love,
Thousand kilograms of screen time,
Twelve thousand kilograms of speed,
You have made me.

Frankie Flack (9)
Mary Elton Primary School, Clevedon

What Makes Me Unique

T iny and I'm rhymy,
H i there, this is me,
I am the only me,
S ee, I'm the only me,

I 'm hyper mode,
S miling every day,

M y crazy! Self,
E ven when I'm sad I'm crazy!

Ella Buttery (8)
Mary Elton Primary School, Clevedon

What I Love And What I Like

I like to play Among Us,
I love soft plays,
I love watching Spider-Man movies,
I like to see my friends,
I love my family,
I like to be at Weston Pier,
I like to eat pizza,
I like fruit,
I like to run around,
I love doing arts and crafts.

James Pearce (9)
Mary Elton Primary School, Clevedon

This Is Happy Me

B est at being happy,
I deas everywhere,
R eading a lot,
T alented at making food,
H appy every day,
D oing drawings is what I love,
A rt is where I belong,
Y ay, it's my birthday next month.

Olivia England (8)
Mary Elton Primary School, Clevedon

Indiana Is Cool!

I am very tall!
N othing I can't do!
D ad, Mum and my brother are who I live with!
I love animals!
A nd I am good at football!
N o food I don't like!
A nd finally I have three BFFs and lots of friends!

Indiana Badger (8)
Mary Elton Primary School, Clevedon

How To Make Me

Always need one million pounds of kindness!
Happiness, sugar everywhere!
Ten footballs and fifteen cats!
One million books!
Loads of sparkles!
McDonald's cheeseburgers! And lots of ice cream!
Friends!
That's how you make me.

Evie Gully (8)
Mary Elton Primary School, Clevedon

Hollie Of The Hearts

H ollie of the hearts,
E yes that glitter in the light,
A s soft as a feather hair,
R ed lips like the sun in the shining light,
T ired every morning like a sloth,
S plashing sweet scents like a flower.

Hollie Hepworth (8)
Mary Elton Primary School, Clevedon

My Name And Me!

S aturday, my favourite day,
I n my bed, I have loads of panda teddies,
E ven though it's ten o'clock I won't get up!
N aughty as an elf,
N o boys allowed in my room,
A nd I love my family.

Sienna Gomm (9)
Mary Elton Primary School, Clevedon

I Can...

A dd big numbers in maths
N ever forget how to play my guitar
D o the fifteen times table
R ide a scooter and a bike
E at a plate full of garlic bread
W alk for hours with my family.

Andrew Liu (8)
Mary Elton Primary School, Clevedon

Making Me

A tablespoon of kindness,
A tablespoon of funny,
A tablespoon of love,
A tablespoon of short,
A tablespoon of maths,
A tablespoon of PS4 games,
A tablespoon of McDonald's, chilling, hugs,
And that is me!

Jaden Cox (8)
Mary Elton Primary School, Clevedon

Football

F unny and crazy,
O nly me, no worries,
O uch, that hurt,
T o the moon,
B ack to the beach,
A lways smiling,
L aughing every day,
L et me be me.

Charlie Henley-Smith (9)
Mary Elton Primary School, Clevedon

Meet Me

M y name is Megan,
E nthusiastic and eager to learn,
G ood at reading and writing,
A rt is where I shine,
N ice to meet you, I hope we can be friends.

Megan Greenway (9)
Mary Elton Primary School, Clevedon

Me Is Me

K ind and caring,
E very day is me,
E ven me is enough,
L aughing every day,
E very day I'm crazy!
Y ou see, I am the only me!

Keeley Johns (9)
Mary Elton Primary School, Clevedon

Kind Rocks

F antastic,
I nterested,
N ice,
L ikes to eat lots of food,
E nergetic,
Y ou can be you and I can be me.

Finley Barrow (8)
Mary Elton Primary School, Clevedon

Make Magic

M indful magic,
A mazing and awesome,
G reat and good,
I magine about magic,
C urious and kind.

Maddie Upton (8)
Mary Elton Primary School, Clevedon

Sam Is...

Sam is kind,
Sam is creative,
Sam is caring,
Sam is playful,
Sam is good at making games up.

Sam Barney (8)
Mary Elton Primary School, Clevedon

This Is Me

On my way to Chamonix, skiing and climbing mountains,
Surfing the waves down in Newquay,
Making sausage rolls and Bakewells with my mum and dad,
Maggie is waiting for me at Red Earth Equestrian Centre,
I love my home-made chicken curry
After my football match on Sunday,
Thursday is the best day for horse riding,
When I get home, my dog is waiting.

Roars in the room as food wafts through the air,
A running family through BL8,
As my dog charges across his favourite field,
Supportive to my dad at Ironman.

Patting Maggie as I canter over the jump,
Being a lightning bolt on right midfield,
Pressuring every Tuesday at Heywood,
A solid defender here.

Ruby Pilling (10)
Old Hall Primary School, Brandlesholme

This Is Me

Walls open to worlds unknown,
Magic flying in the air, wands and robes everywhere,
The golden trio, fight side by side forever,
But not all's good when he comes... you know who,
Then the TV turns off and all's back to normal in the real world.

She's annoying but I love her,
They're sweet and kind, two parents of a kind,
A mum, a dad, a sister, they're all the best, nothing like the rest,
When we're together, it's the best.

I love to read from top to bottom, never missing a word,
Singing and dancing are what I do,
Red, orange, yellow make me happy,
But my favourite thing is to doodle and sketch.

Saraih Jakeway-Couser (10)
Old Hall Primary School, Brandlesholme

This Is Me

Animals all around the house,
Snakes linger in the kitchen, waiting for their daily meal,
Mice on the menu today,
I open my eyes, to my surprise I'm surrounded by two ginger furballs,
The purring sounds act as my morning alarm.

Roars from every room for football and rugby,
Balls flying through the garden,
No dirty tackles here,
Picnics on the hill and berry picking next to the bell tower.

Birds chirping as the pitter-patter of feet grows quieter,
Water gushing from a high cliff,
Guitar strings humming as the pick flies across the body,
Acoustic guitars stand proudly in the living room.

Dylan de Jager (11)
Old Hall Primary School, Brandlesholme

This Is Me

The sound of splashing in the pool,
Bounce, bounce on the trampoline,
Climbing like a monkey,
High up in the trees,
Birds chirping to the pitter-patter of feet,
The strings of guitar making noise.

My brother banging his controller,
My sister running around,
Me watching Netflix,
My parents chilling, reading books,
The dog playing in the garden,
The cat taking a nap.

An ambition to rule the law,
Help and assist where I can,
Handcuffs at the ready,
A role model I will be.

Eliza Goodier (11)
Old Hall Primary School, Brandlesholme

This Is Me!

I'm a powerful hitter on the court,
Determined to win the matches when I play,
I play shooter games and I love to draw,
I also watch Marvel movies in my spare time.

I have two pets named Buddy and Oscar,
One's a cat and the other is a dog,
We take Buddy out for daily walks,
While Oscar roams around the neighbourhood.

A future awaits in London,
Home of the biggest tournament in the world,
And competing in many more,
With my goal in sight, Wimbledon glory.

Max Lindley (10)
Old Hall Primary School, Brandlesholme

This Is Me

A midfield masterclass,
A passion for winning,
A strong leader on the grass,
Encouragement is important,
We share the same goal,
Success and enjoyment.

When Saturday comes, I see my dad,
We play games together,
A console and controller get our attention together,
And concentration fills the room.

Ambitions to play professional football,
Dedication needed every week,
School remains my focus,
But the dream excites me.

Zach Mehers (11)
Old Hall Primary School, Brandlesholme

This Is Me

Living with two brothers, both teach me,
My sister's a nurse,
Mum and Dad are great,
No pets in my home, only a fish.

Football is my passion,
I play whenever I can,
Mosque is priority,
Balance in my life is very key.

I have a Nintendo Switch and PS4,
Gaming is never a chore,
Cricket in the local park,
But not when it's dark.
In bed for nine,
To be ready for the new day to shine.

Shuraim Khan (11)
Old Hall Primary School, Brandlesholme

This Is Me

A boy between the poles who saves a lot of goals,
A passion for winning and I'm cool for fashion,
Shouting at the defenders, watch offside,
Taking accurate goal kicks to help us get up the pitch.

Family are important to me, two brothers and mum and dad,
Two dogs are our company, mealtimes are fun, yet hectic.

Jokes are a passion of mine, entertaining is icy,
Selling out arenas,
This is the dream.

McKinley Haslam (10)
Old Hall Primary School, Brandlesholme

This Is Me

I am a wall in defence,
Me, a baseball lover,
Gaming brings me joy,
Winning is the icing on the cake.

My mum is loving and caring,
My dad plays FIFA with me,
My grandma spoils me daily,
My auntie makes a big feast,
My cousins play with me,
I'm so fortunate for family.

The future Sherlock Holmes,
A future war hero,
Either way I help people,
I want to solve mysteries.

Harry Nolan (10)
Old Hall Primary School, Brandlesholme

This Is Me

Hair like fire,
Swims like an axolotl,
Jumping on a trampoline like a frog,
Drawing skills a ten,
Skateboarding down the streets,
Having fun.

A big family,
Two little sisters,
An older stepbrother,
Two younger stepsisters,
Parents and two parents,
A dog and two cats.

Every Sunday morning,
Scoring goals with a stick,
People cheering,
On the pitch.

Charlotte Goldsbrough (10)
Old Hall Primary School, Brandlesholme

This Is Me

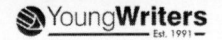

I look at my inventions every day,
To armour, to swords and helmets too.

I play games like Fortnite and even Minecraft,
I'm the best at making spaceships and winning Fortnite matches.

I also do art, anime and Avengers,
I make sculptures of caricatures, movies and more,
I make lights work, motors turn and everything else.

I'm creative and crafty with everything I do.

Jackson Brown (10)
Old Hall Primary School, Brandlesholme

This Is Me!

Catching what comes my way,
Focusing on the bowler's delivery,
A keeper of wicket,
Biking down vast valleys,
Playing with friends and family.

Two siblings in the house,
Blonde hair, blue eyes,
A mother and a father,
All living together.

Soon I'll be going to high school,
Facing all my fears,
Pursuing all my dreams,
Peddling, walking, swimming.

Harry Nuttall (10)
Old Hall Primary School, Brandlesholme

This Is Me

Tackles of many,
Tastes of them all,
A passion for sports,
Manchester United's biggest fan.

Playing FIFA, scoring goals,
Potting all the balls, king of the pool table,
Hanging out with friends.

One brother, one sister,
Annoying as can be.
Spending time at two different houses.
Tennis with my dad,
Drawing with my mum,
Fighting with my siblings.

Zayn Sultan-Smethurst (10)
Old Hall Primary School, Brandlesholme

This Is Me

A set-piece specialist,
Sharing quality time with the team,
Brave in tackles always,
And rapid down the wings.

My hobby is art,
I wish to be an architect,
But I'm not so smart,
But hard work awaits me.

I have one little sister,
Who just learned how to walk,
And hopefully soon she will learn how to talk,
My name is Rocco, I am ten years old.

Rocco Sharpe (10)
Old Hall Primary School, Brandlesholme

This Is Me

I like dancing,
A passion for winning,
I like to be front and centre,
Sharing victory and losses.

I have a sibling at the house,
I love my dog and taking him on walks,
I have a mother and father,
And I also enjoy painting.

I'd love to become a dance teacher,
On stage, bowing to the audience,
And my friends on stage with me.

Matilda Rose Hargreaves (10)
Old Hall Primary School, Brandlesholme

This Is Me

My family is my safe spot,
We always look out for each other,
I love to play out,
Spend time with my friends,
Minecraft and Roblox online,
I hope this will never end.

I am ten years old,
An adventurous nature,
I love to go on walks, especially in the woods,
Reading is my favourite thing,
Lots of pictures drawn.

Isabella Anne Lord (10)
Old Hall Primary School, Brandlesholme

This Is Me

My family and I play board games,
I'm very competitive,
I don't want to lose,
Colour brain on the table ready to play.

I colour print pictures,
Google my inspiration,
I grab my pencil and let it flow,
Paying close attention to every detail,
Even when it comes to Simba's tail.

Ava Challender (10)
Old Hall Primary School, Brandlesholme

This Is Me

A love for shopping,
A listening ear for others,
Shy when there are lots of people,
Loving my close friends!

Three fishy friends live in a tank,
Wish they were giraffes,
I think they would get stuck!
Can't have a cat,
Might eat the fish,
Animal lover forever.

Faziah Ahmed (11)
Old Hall Primary School, Brandlesholme

This Is Me

I like listening to K-pop,
Glasses suit me well,
Swimming is a passion,
Dinosaurs interest me.

Family are my life,
My mother is caring,
My brother is my friend,
Two cats comfort us.

A future YouTuber in the making.

Mollimae Brown (11)
Old Hall Primary School, Brandlesholme

How To Make Me

M ix in a blue bottle some kindness, friendship and love,
A purple bottle has luck in it, so mix all of that in,
K indness is the most important thing to add, so mix lots in,
E xcitement and adventure are my favourite things, mix them up to make a great person.

M ix up all the tinyness so I am small,
E xciting things will happen when you mix all of them up with a spell I made, without it it will not work, after all the hard work.

Isabel Quinn (8)
Smarden Primary School, Smarden

I Am... Rosie Gray

R abbits are cute and so are you.
O ranges are orange and so are autumn leaves.
S nakes have no legs, neither do fish.
I gloos are white and so is snow.
E ggs crack and so does bubble wrap.

G rass is green
R ainbows are pretty and so am I.
A pples are red and so is lipstick.
Y aks are big and so are killer whales.

Rosie Gray (7)
Smarden Primary School, Smarden

My Recipe

A pinch of kindness,
A dose of laughter,
A spoonful of fidget,
Throw in a length of swimming,
Two spoonfuls of persuasiveness,
A shake of braveness,
Pour in two cups of friendship,
Five cups of playfulness,
Pour five grams of love,
Throw in some niceness.

Pearl Crowe (7)
Smarden Primary School, Smarden

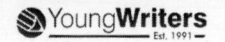

What You Need To Be Me

Find two hundred kilograms of kindness, get two sparkling eyes.

Make five drops of helpfulness,
Get twenty kits of sugar,
Find nineteen bits of love,
Make seven pinches of being very kind,
Eight drops of kind words,
And finally two drops of friendliness.

Lizzie Waldock (7)
Smarden Primary School, Smarden

About Me

I am as quick as a cheetah,
As good as a professional gamer,
My legs can run one hundred miles per hour,
My arms are as strong as a strong man,
I can climb so high,
And good at being kind,
Love my family and friends,
Love making stories.

George Etheridge (9)
Smarden Primary School, Smarden

My Cat Cookie

Cookie is a calm, cute, cat.
Cookie has a fuzzy and fluffy hat.
Cookie might get the best rest at night.
Cookie has a very loving heart.
Cookie is really smart.
Cookie will give you a warm lap.
Cookie can drink from the tap.
Cookie will spring up, it will give you a ping.
Cookie you will never forget because he's so loving.
Cookie is a bit chunky but he can be a little selfish.
Cookie can be lazy but he can be crazy.
Cookie is that fast you can't see him pass.
Cookie is messy but he can be funny.
Cookie is picky, however, he can be very sneaky.
Cookie does always land on his feet.

Sofia Kowal (9)
St Cuthbert's Primary School, Glasgow

Sadness

Sadness never says anything, his loneliness makes him more sad.
Sad is shy but he might just say hi.
When sadness cries, it's like a waterfall with a splash.
Sadness is not anger, he is just sad, he does not shout, he cries.
If you give him a cuddle, he will join the huddle.
Sadness will have friendly friends, he will be loyal and get a cuddle.
Sadness will not be lonely, he will not feel cold inside, he will feel warm and happy.
Sadness is always okay but talking to friends will make his day.
Sadness' heart will be as warm as lava.
His smile will reach the sky.

Patience Asemota (9)
St Cuthbert's Primary School, Glasgow

My Big Brother

My big brother is very tall and very funny.
When he is mad he gets very grumpy.
He is always annoying but he often enjoys his cake.
My brother has big black eyes.
His big eyes help him to see things.
He runs very fast so that you can't see him running past.
He works very hard and his art pieces are fantastic.
He is very sneaky by taking away my art pieces.
He is very cheeky when he cheats.
His room is always messy but he is very stressy.
He helps me when I am sad and makes me happy.
He is always in a hurry because he always has so many things to do.

Jenna Chi (9)
St Cuthbert's Primary School, Glasgow

My Dream Job

M acy's Meals is the name of my great restaurant.
Y ou like yummy, fantastic food? Well, we got it.

D icing cucumber for a fabulous summer salad.
R are meals you can only get here.
E ating steak that is pan-fried.
A meal is as good as the sweetest strawberry on a summer day.
M aking meals makes me feel confident.

J ust cooking makes me happy, it brings me joy.
O h, there's the pot, the king of the kitchen.
B rilliant food made by Macy, the super chef.

Macy Louise Green (10)
St Cuthbert's Primary School, Glasgow

My Big Sister

My sister is really good at skating but when she goes ice skating she is always waiting.
My sister is very smart and excellent at art.
My sister's hair is messy and her wardrobe is really dressy.
My sister is super funny but she has a little bit of money.
My sister is sweet and when I go to the shops she always buys me a treat.
My sister is so fun in the very hot sun.
My sister is so joyful that she is very loyal.
My sister is really lovely like a flower in a vase.

Elizabeth Aiwekhoe (8)
St Cuthbert's Primary School, Glasgow

My Favourite Teddy

Bunny is friendly and her clothes very trendy.
She is a sweet bunny with the sweetest heart.
Sometimes I put her in a little cart.
Bunny is soft, so she can't sleep in the loft.
Sometimes Bunny is lost, sometimes she isn't, three or four times she went missing.
Bunny doesn't live under rocks but she likes sneaking into socks.
Bunny doesn't like treats but she likes sneaking into the cupboard and stealing all the sweets.

Sara Carbin (9)
St Cuthbert's Primary School, Glasgow

Summertime

When the day is young you can have fun in the sun.
You can go to the beach and have a peach.
The flowers flourish big and bright, it's such a delight.
When the sun sets and the sky is clear, if lucky, you'll see a deer.
In the forest, while warm, you will see a swarm.
When the moon has risen, the view is breathtaking but you need vision.
I love summer and if you stay inside you're just a bummer.

Nadia Cudjoe (9)
St Cuthbert's Primary School, Glasgow

Gaming

In gaming you need a keyboard to play or else you will have to play on mobile.
Gaming makes me warm like my tummy in a storm.
Gaming in the sun makes me feel like I'm sitting on a tree palm.
You can game for very long, it will make your fingers very strong.
Gaming can be challenging but sometimes can be easy,
You need to stop when you get sneezy.

Aleksander Jagielski (9)
St Cuthbert's Primary School, Glasgow

The... Grows Happily

The plant grows happily because
The fresh sun sees grass and plants.

The tree grows happily because
The trees make a forest to talk with you.

The water flows happily because
The booming tasty water is being sipped.

The fruit tastes happily because
The juicy water is within it.

The vegetables taste happily because
It makes you healthy and strong like a gym master.

Michael Odigie (10)
St Cuthbert's Primary School, Glasgow

Moviemakers

Moviemakers are amazing,
They often have people glaring.
Their art is off the chart,
It leaves a stamp on my heart.
They travel around the world,
Their hair is often curled.
Moviemakers are the best,
I tried to study for my test.
They have lots of money,
But they're always in a hurry.

Tyler Redmond (9)
St Cuthbert's Primary School, Glasgow

This Is Football

Footballers have to be fit, they also have to wear a kit.
Footballers kick a ball that hits a wall.
You cannot see them pass because they are so fast.
Footballers are super tall, that's why they're good at kicking the ball.
In the sun they find it easy but they find it challenging when it's breezy.

Lennon Brereton (9)
St Cuthbert's Primary School, Glasgow

What To Fix

I want to fix the hamster that runs like a panther,
I want to fix the fox who was found in a box,
I want to fix the dog who hurt his leg on a log,
He was found in a bog,
I want to fix the mouse who fell in the house,
I want to fix the sheep who had difficulty to sleep.

Lily Mae Gurney (8)
St Cuthbert's Primary School, Glasgow

Leading The Way

I want to be a leader because I am a keen reader.
I want to make the law as people are in awe.
I won't fall in a ditch because I am rich.
I want to make people happy because they are sappy.
I want to lead the way so everyone can stay.

Martins Omonijo (8)
St Cuthbert's Primary School, Glasgow

The Frightening Dog Star

When I saw a hamster,
There was a gangster.
He sang like a star
I gave my friend a snack bar,
And he called me a bronze star
And my friend bought me a flat car,
And there was a giant dog star
And I screamed! Very loud.

Kingsley Odigie (8)
St Cuthbert's Primary School, Glasgow

My Dream

Scientists are smart and they sometimes do art.
Scientists are not taken for a fool.
They cure diseases, so you don't sneeze.
I am so clever, my experiments make me shiver.
It is often dangerous, so I need to be outrageous.

River Warren (8)
St Cuthbert's Primary School, Glasgow

Super Ball

I am fit and I like to train quite a bit,
When I win my head goes in a spin,
I kick a ball, sometimes I fall,
I always cheer with my peers,
I am a footballer, I always make the dollar,
I am a footballer.

Declan Atkins (8)
St Cuthbert's Primary School, Glasgow

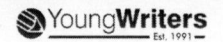

I Like To Find

I like to find bones with stones but my mum often moans.
I like to find thrones but they are often a phone.
I like to dig with twigs but I often find wigs.
I like to find gold but I often find old mould.

Tiernan Warren (8)
St Cuthbert's Primary School, Glasgow

The Day I Saved A Goal

I saved the ball because I am tall,
I make the saves because I am brave,
When I save there is a cold wave,
When it hits the top bar I jump far,
When I throw I say go,
When I throw I say go.

Hevar Karimi (8)
St Cuthbert's Primary School, Glasgow

Winter

W inter is cold,
I n the snow it will always glow.
N ovember is cold,
T he snow is always bold.
E very winter I see glitter,
R eady for a snowball fight.

Hanna Rekas (8)
St Cuthbert's Primary School, Glasgow

A Dancer

A dancer often does the tricks,
They sometimes spin sticks.
They love to move and always groove.
They are super fit and wear sparkly kits.
Because I am a dancer.
Because I am a dancer.

Lacey Sutherland (8)
St Cuthbert's Primary School, Glasgow

I Am A Dancer

I am a dramatic dancer
As graceful as a swan
Running and shouting
I am a leaping lyricist
As fast as a flash
Jumping and swaying
I am a stylish street dancer
As fiery as a flame
Turning and stamping.

Sophie Morgan (10)
St Cuthbert's Primary School, Glasgow

A Gymnast

Often they are fit when they're in a kit,
You twist and turn till you feel the burn,
Sometimes I hurt my hips because I love to flip,
Gymnastics is cool when we spring in a pool.

Lexi Stewart (8)
St Cuthbert's Primary School, Glasgow

My Dream Is Football

Whenever I kick the ball I fall,
Whenever I dribble I see someone nibble,
Whenever I see someone run quick, they always fall over a brick,
Whenever I see a flag I swing my kit bag.

Darren Docherty (8)
St Cuthbert's Primary School, Glasgow

Space

I want to go to space but I will have to wear a brace.
It is a good place to have a race.
The rocket is very fast, I hope I am not last.
I would love to go to space to be ace.

Charlie Clarke (8)
St Cuthbert's Primary School, Glasgow

Love Hair And Make-Up

I love to do hair,
So people stare.
I love to do make-up pop,
So it can help me to get a pup,
I collect lots of bits and bobs,
To create outfits that look amazing.

Keira-Rose Mullen (8)
St Cuthbert's Primary School, Glasgow

Running Fast

When I run fast I have a blast,
When I run like lightning I can be frightening,
When I run quick I can be sick,
When I run slow the wind helps me go.

Jack Chen (8)
St Cuthbert's Primary School, Glasgow

I Am Me

I am smart because I take part.
I am fast and I never come last.
I am pretty and sometimes I am witty.
I am cheeky and sneaky.
I am me.

Poppy Johnston (8)
St Cuthbert's Primary School, Glasgow

My Dad's Car

My dad's car is fast,
You couldn't pass,
My dad's car is black as night,
It has two bright lights.

Junior Hendren (9)
St Cuthbert's Primary School, Glasgow

Doctor

A doctor, a doctor is smart,
A doctor will help your heart.
A doctor is kind,
An illness they will find.

Milena Bednarz (7)
St Cuthbert's Primary School, Glasgow

This Is Me

To create me you will need:
A bedroom full of dogs,
A sprinkle of greatness,
Ten pounds of mischief and happiness,
A bucket full of pepperoni pizza,
A dash of confidence,
A pinch of fierceness and loudness,
Two cups of overprotectiveness,
And one leader.
Now you need to:
Mix all the ingredients together until it's thick and smooth,
Then put in the oven for half an hour and check if it's perfect,
If not, put it back in the oven and if so, sprinkle some loveness on too and let it set.

Hollie Longbottom (9)
Westwood Primary School, Leeds

What Is It?

It's as vicious as a tiger,
As fast as Messi,
As brave as a lion,
It has blue marble eyes,
Their eyes are better than our eyes,
They're as tall as a table,
They're yellow with black spots on their skin,
They're terrified of water,
It's very overprotective,
It's an endangered species,
It is a part of the lion family,
It lives in a warm climate,
What is it?

Answer: A cheetah.

Jon-Paul Massey (10)
Westwood Primary School, Leeds

This Is Me

Sienna is my name!
My dream is to become a lovely, excellent football player,
I would look good in my football boots,
Lightning as bright as lightning bolts.
To be me you will need:
A sprinkle of love,
Pinch of kindness and a slab of brightness.
I am even braver as a scary bear,
Please don't forget that I am faster and more furious than a cheetah or a lion.

Sienna Faith Thornton (9)
Westwood Primary School, Leeds

This Is Me

T his is my dog,
H is name is Bruce,
I don't like it when he likes my sister,
S he is as cute as a puppy.

I love her so much,
S he is the cutest thing that ever happened to me.

M e and my five-year-old sister,
E very one of my siblings love each other so much.

Lacey Mai Prince (9)
Westwood Primary School, Leeds

This Is Me

A pinch of fun,
A handful of love,
As brave as a bear,
A teaspoon of kindness,
A bucket of care,
A gallon of fun.

As kind as a kitten,
As nice as a mitten,
Always funny,
To give people money,
I don't like scratches,
Or matches.

Chloe Mead (10)
Westwood Primary School, Leeds

Charlie

C onfident is what I am,
H yper every day,
A lways trying new things,
R oblox is my favourite game,
L emonade is my favourite drink,
I love my family,
E veryone likes that I am kind.

Charlie Smith (8)
Westwood Primary School, Leeds

Imogen

I love drawing,
M y favourite subject is art,
O n a walk I bring my dogs,
G ive and share, that's what I do,
E lephants are my things,
N ow I'm done, you can be my friends.

Imogen Cardiss (9)
Westwood Primary School, Leeds

This Is Me
A kennings poem

I am an...
Astronomy explorer,
Spider hater,
Cat lover,
Dog lover,
Winter wisher,
Pizza craver,
Book reader,
Artist,
Nature lover,
Gamer,
And finally...
A good person.

Casey Marie Clements (10)
Westwood Primary School, Leeds

This Is Peter

P olite to lots of people,
E njoy learning at school,
T angerines are my favourite fruit,
E lephants are my favourite animal because I love them,
R espectful to loads of people.

Peter Folkes (8)
Westwood Primary School, Leeds

This Is Alfie

A pple juice is my favourite drink,
L ooney is what I am,
F ood is my favourite thing in the world,
I enjoy being with my friends,
E nergy, I have too much.

Alfie Beanland (9)
Westwood Primary School, Leeds

This Is Me!
A kennings poem

I am a...
YouTube watcher,
Wasp hater,
Footballer,
Family lover,
Sausage roll eater,
Winter wisher,
Heavy sleeper,
Late riser,
And finally...
A good baker.

Fabian Bundy (11)
Westwood Primary School, Leeds

This Is Freya

F unny sometimes,
R iding bikes with my daddy at the weekends,
E njoy cooking tea with my mummy,
Y ou can always count on me,
A mazing student in maths.

Freya Ward (9)
Westwood Primary School, Leeds

This Is Me
A kennings poem

I am a,
Leeds supporter,
PS4 player,
Football watcher,
Footballer,
Pasta eater,
FIFA lover,
Heavy sleeper,
Sweet eater,
And finally,
A good listener.

Alfie Opie (11)
Westwood Primary School, Leeds

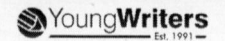

This Is Riley

R iley, yes, it's Riley,
I like apple juice,
L ike a tiger but never roar,
E ating is my favourite thing to do,
Y o, I'm so silly, bro.

Riley Smith (9)
Westwood Primary School, Leeds

This Is Koby

K ing of maths,
O bviously, I like McDonald's,
B eing a lunatic at home,
Y ou won't believe how fast I am at football.

Koby Lucas Bransberg Kirk (8)
Westwood Primary School, Leeds

This Is Mia R

M e and my sister love drawing,
I am intelligent,
A mazing at schoolwork.

R ely on me for anything.

Mia Rush (9)
Westwood Primary School, Leeds

This Is Me

You can count on me,
I like to ride on my BMX,
Elephants are my favourite animal,
Singing in music lessons is my favourite.

Myles White (10)
Westwood Primary School, Leeds

All About Xavier

A kennings poem

Football smasher,
Joke giver,
Scooter jumper,
Game player,
Art designer,
Courageous thinker.

Xavier Mead (7)
Westwood Primary School, Leeds

All About Porchia
A kennings poem

Dance lover,
Football player,
Car passenger,
Joker giver,
Smart sister,
Scooter hopper.

Porchia Last (7)
Westwood Primary School, Leeds

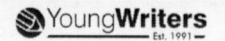

All About Carter
A kennings poem

Game player,
Football player,
Rugby tackler,
Happy speeder,
Art lover,
Brave dancer.

Carter Prince (7)
Westwood Primary School, Leeds

All About Charlie
A kennings poem

Train lover,
Car passenger,
Lego lover,
Art lover,
Game player,
Confused thinker.

Charlie Green (7)
Westwood Primary School, Leeds

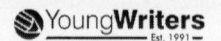

All About Abbie

A kennings poem

Baton twirler,
Art lover,
Clumsy farmer,
Dance skipper,
Game player,
Joke giver.

Abbie Burdon (7)
Westwood Primary School, Leeds

All About Isla
A kennings poem

Baby lover,
Baton twirler,
Brave holder,
Art lover,
Train watcher,
Dance lover.

Isla Cockcroft (7)
Westwood Primary School, Leeds

All About TreydenThomas
A kennings poem

Rugby player,
Dance goer,
Train goer,
Game player,
Scooter rider,
Joke giver.

TreydenThomas Appleyard (7)
Westwood Primary School, Leeds

All About Tisha

A kennings poem

Dance lover,
Art lover,
Game player,
Neat writer.

Tisha Z Kakunguwo (7)
Westwood Primary School, Leeds

YOUNG WRITERS INFORMATION

We hope you have enjoyed reading this book – and that you will continue to in the coming years.

If you're the parent or family member of an enthusiastic poet or story writer, do visit our website **www.youngwriters.co.uk/subscribe** and sign up to receive news, competitions, writing challenges and tips, activities and much, much more! There's lots to keep budding writers motivated!

If you would like to order further copies of this book, or any of our other titles, then please give us a call or order via your online account.

Young Writers
Remus House
Coltsfoot Drive
Peterborough
PE2 9BF
(01733) 890066
info@youngwriters.co.uk

Join in the conversation!
Tips, news, giveaways and much more!

YoungWritersUK **YoungWritersCW** **youngwriterscw**